FloridaOneTankTrips.com

FLORIDA ONE TANK TRIPS
VOLUME 1

Fifty Nifty Places You Can Visit On One Tank Of Gas

Second Edition 2017

Mike Miller

INTRODUCTION

As this book is published in 2016, many families cannot afford the steep admission fees for a day or two at the major theme parks such as Walt Disney World, Universal Studios Florida, and SeaWorld. A family of four can typically find it costs them more than $400 just to get in and a huge amount on top of that for food and drink and extra attractions once they are inside.

Florida One Tank Trips Volume 1 fills the need for a handy directory to more affordable attractions, all within a one tank drive of one of six major Florida cities: Jacksonville, Miami, Orlando, Pensacola, Tallahassee and Tampa.

Each attraction in the book is described and includes information on admission fees, operating hours, and contact information including address, telephone number and website.

Volume 1 features 50 of these attractions. Future volumes in this series will cover even more of them.

You will find yourself having a lot of fun and saving a lot of money.

AUTHOR

Mike Miller has lived in Florida since 1960. He graduated from the University of Florida with a degree in civil engineering and has lived and worked in most areas of Florida. His projects include Walt Disney World, EPCOT, Universal Studios and hundreds of commercial, municipal and residential developments all over the state.

During that time, Mike developed an understanding and love of Old Florida that is reflected in the pages of his website, **Florida-Backroads-Travel.com.**

If you have enjoyed this book and purchased it on **Amazon**, Mike would appreciate it if you would take a couple of minutes to post a short review at Amazon. Thoughtful reviews help other customers make better buying choices. He reads all of his reviews personally, and each one helps him write better books in the future. Thanks for your support!

FLORIDA'S 8 GEOGRAPHICAL REGIONS

TABLE OF CONTENTS

ORLANDO AND CENTRAL FLORIDA

TAMPA AND WEST FLORIDA

PENSACOLA AND NORTHWEST FLORIDA

TALLAHASSEE AND NORTH CENTRAL FLORIDA

JACKSONVILLE AND NORTHEAST FLORIDA

MIAMI AND SOUTHEAST FLORIDA

ANCIENT SPANISH MONASTERY

The monastery was actually built in Spain in 1141. It was purchased by William Randolph Hearst, taken apart and shipped to America, and finally ended up here in North Miami Beach. The building is more than 400 years older than some of the national historic monuments in St. Augustine.

The buildings and grounds are beautiful, and have become a popular place for weddings and other special ceremonies. Church services are held on Sundays and weekdays.

BASIC INFORMATION

16711 West Dixie Highway

North Miami Beach, Florida 33160

Tel: 305-945-1461

spanishmonastery.com

Admission Fees: $10/adult, $5/students and seniors

Hours: Mon-Sat 1000 am - 430pm, Sunday 1100 am - 430 pm

BABCOCK RANCH ECO-TOURS

Babcock Ranch Eco-Tours is a once in a lifetime opportunity that takes place on a working 92,000 acre ranch that is typical of what Old Florida was all about. Florida has a historic tradition of having large cattle ranches, and this is one of them.

This is a ranch where you may see an endangered Florida panther in its wild home, and you will see the tough bulls and cows unique to Florida known as Cracker cattle. The way you will see most of this ranch is on their Swamp Buggy Tour that takes an hour and a half. You can even have your lunch at the ranch by bringing you own or enjoy an onsite restaurant.

BASIC INFORMATION

8000 Florida State Road 31

Punta Gorda, Florida 33982

Tel: 1-800-500-5583

BabcockRanchEcoTours.com

Winter Tours: Nov 1-Apr 30, 10am-3pm,7 days/week

Adults $24, Children 3-12, $16, 2 and under free

Summer Tours: May 1-Oct 30, 10am-2pm, Wed-Sunday

Adults: $22, Children 3-12, $12, 2 and under free

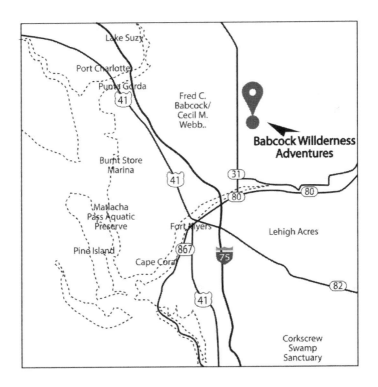

BOK TOWER GARDENS

The quiet gardens and serenity of Bok Tower is a pleasant contrast to all of the busy activity of the theme parks in Orlando and elsewhere in Central Florida. This attraction is only one hour from Orlando but it seems far away from the traffic.

Edward Bok was the editor of the Ladies Home Journal and transformed this sandy hill near Lake Wales into one of the most beautiful places in the country. The tropical plantings give shade to visitors and home to more than 100 species of birds.

The singing tower with its carillon plays concerts every day at 100 pm and 300 pm, and shorter musical pieces at other times during the day. Bok Tower Gardens has also become one of Florida' most popular spots for weddings.

BASIC INFORMATION

1151 Tower Blvd

Lake Wales, Florida 33853

Tel: 863-676-1408

boktowergardens.org

Admission Fees: Adults $20, Children $10

Hours: Open 365 days/year from 800 am to 600 pm

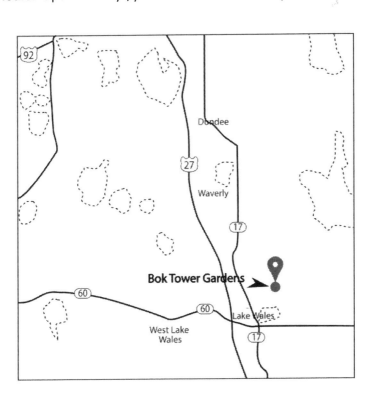

BREVARD ZOO

The small Brevard Zoo is one of the most popular zoos in Florida. Visitors will enjoy more than 165 species that include more than 550 different animals creatively housed on 22 acres of restored wetlands. Animals in the zoo are from Florida, Asia, Africa, Australia and South America. One of the fun ways to see the zoo is via a guided kayak tour.

One of the features of this zoo is that you are allowed to feed animals such as the giraffes and the birds and can enjoy being up close and personal while riding a miniature train around the grounds through the animal's natural habitat. Over 16,000 volunteers helped to build this zoo and their love and care still shows.

You can also purchase special tickets at the zoo that give you a one of a kind experience such as going kayaking, have an encounter with a rhino, enjoy the petting zoo, renting a paddle boat and dozens of other such adventures.

There are numerous special events and school field trips during the year as well.

BASIC INFORMATION

8225 North Wickham Road
Melbourne, Florida 32940
Tel: 321-823-3767
brevardzoo.org

Admission Fee: Adults $19.95, Children 3-11 $14.95, Children Under 3 Free.

Hours: Open Daily 930 am – 500 pm, last admission at 415 pm.

CASSADAGA SPIRITUALIST CAMP

This historic old town has preserved its original roots as a spiritualist camp. This is a town where several psychics and mediums live and still ply their craft. There are many Victorian era cottages and homes in the camp where the spiritualists live and work.

There are 40 certified mediums in the village, and also a large number of healers who pride themselves on teaching people to tap into their own ability to heal themselves. A hotel on site is reportedly home to ghosts, and there is a gift shop with crystals, stones, jewelry, DVDs and CDs and a large collection of books on spiritualism and metaphysics.

The entire village is on the National Register of Historic Places.

BASIC INFORMATION

355 Cassadaga Road

Cassadaga, Florida 32744

(This is the address of the Cassadaga Hotel)

cassadaga.org for information on events

Admission Fees: Admission to the camp/village is free.

Individual mediums and other services priced separately.

Hours: Open 365 days/year

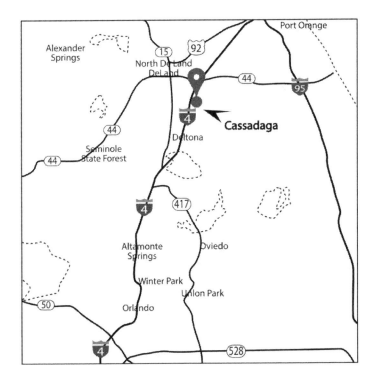

CHATTAWAY RESTAURANT

This old Florida establishment has been serving casual diners in St. Petersburg for more than 90 years. It features outside dining and is a favorite of the locals. Tourists have a bit harder time finding it because it is not in the neighborhood of marinas and museums that most visitors to St. Pete are interested in.

The main decorating item in this restaurant's décor is the claw foot bathtub. They are everywhere your eye takes you and are used as planters for a botanical treasure of exotic flowers and tropical plants.

The most famous dish here is the 7 ounce hamburger loaded with everything you want and named the Chattaburger. There are other menu items, of course, like salads and chili and they also serve beer and wine.

Just remember to bring some cash because they don't take credit cards. There is an ATM on site in case you forget.

BASIC INFORMATION

358 22nd Avenue S.
St. Petersburg, Florida 33705
Tel: 727-823-1594

Admission Fees: Free. Menu prices vary.

Hours: Monday-Friday, 1100 am – 930 pm. Saturday and
Sunday 1100 am – 1000 pm.

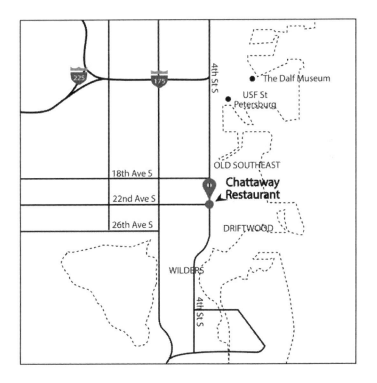

CHAUTAUQUA VINEYARDS

This vineyard and winery is named after the Chautauqua Assembly in New York state that chose nearby DeFuniak Springs as its southern headquarters from 1885 to 1928. The vineyards are more recent than that, but offer a great experience after you've spent the days exploring the Victorian wonders of the town.

Established in 1979, the 40 acre vineyard and winery opened for business in 1990. The grapes grown in the vineyard are Muscadine, and the wine is only sold here at the winery or in a nearby shop in Destin named Emerald Coast Wine Cellars.

The winery is open for tours and tastings every day, and is also the scene of many music festivals and special events.

BASIC INFORMATION

364 Hugh Adams Road

DeFuniak Springs, Florida 32435

Tel: 850-892-5887

chautauquawinery.com

Admission Fees: Free plus free wine tasting

Hours: Open Daily 900 am to 500 pm

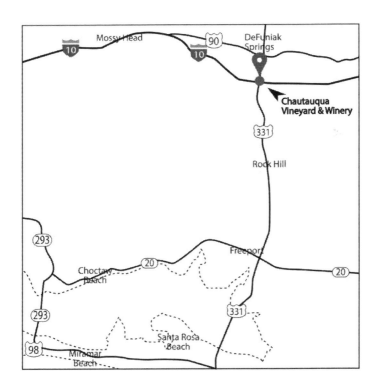

CITRUS TOWER

The Florida Citrus Tower opened in 1956 and was a major tourist attraction in the years before Walt Disney World opened. From its observation deck 22 stories above the ground, it offered views of thousands of acres of citrus and lakes that dominated Central Florida.

These days the view is more of roof tops, but you can still see the lakes, downtown Orlando, Walt Disney World and many other attractions after taking the elevator to the top.

BASIC INFORMATION

141 North US Highway 27
Clermont, Florida 34711
Tel: 352-394-4061
citrustower.com

Admission Fees: Adults $6.00, Children 3-15 $4.00, Children younger than 3, Free

Hours: Monday-Saturday, 900 am – 500 pm. Closed on Sundays Thanksgiving and Christmas

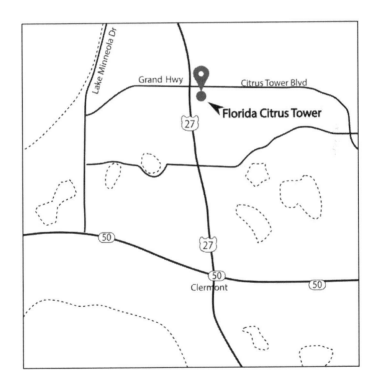

CLARK'S FISH CAMP

Clark's Fish Camp is located south of Jacksonville on Julington Creek in Mandarin. You will not see any seafood restaurant in Florida quite like this one. It is truly unique and has been entertaining people with good food and atmosphere for decades.

The food is good, but the interior is what attracts people. It is stuffed with what may well be the world's largest privately owned taxidermy collection. You will be dining next to lifelike stuffed panthers, lions, deer, fish, birds and even alligators.

In addition to the taxidermy collection, you can watch a daily alligator feeding. This event usually takes place at 630 pm and features the restaurant's own alligator, Lilly. She lives in a comfortable glass cage and people waiting for their dinner table enjoy watching her lying there minding her own business.

Seafood is the big thing on Clark's menu and you can find just about anything from the sea you might want. Enjoy oysters, catfish, mahi mahi, trout, crawfish, frog legs and much more. If you are a landlubber, you can choose from a wide selection of beef offerings. Clark's also has a full liquor bar.

BASIC INFORMATION

12903 Hood Landing Road
Jacksonville, Florida 32258
Tel: 904-268-3474
clarksfishcamp.com

Admission: Free, Menu Prices Vary

Hours: Monday-Thursday, 430 pm-900 pm, Friday 430 pm-1000 pm, Saturday 1100 am- 000 pm, Sunday 1130 am-900 pm

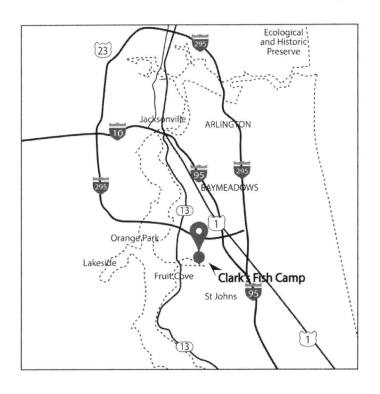

CORAL CASTLE

A young Latvian man named Ed Leedskalnin was about to be married to his 16 year old sweetheart but she backed out the day before the wedding. Ed was broken hearted and left the Old Country for America and ended up in Florida in 1918. He decided to create a permanent monument to his sweetheart and started work on his castle.

Ed was only five feet tall and weighed about 100 pounds. This is something that will amaze you when you see the size of the giant rocks that he used to build his monument. Somehow he did it and with absolutely no help from anybody else. He carved 1100 tons of coral rock and moved them into locations on his property. He had no large machinery, and he did most of his work after sunset using kerosene lanterns for light.

Each section of the wall at Coral Castle is 8 feet tall, 4 feet wide and 3 feet thick. Ed died without ever revealing the mystery of how he was able to manipulate these giant rocks. He only said he understood the law of gravity and the use of leverage. Engineers are still mystified that Ed was able to do this.

19

BASIC INFORMATION

28655 South Dixie Highway
Homestead, Florida 33033
Tel: 305-248-6345
coralcastle.com

Admission Fees: Adults $18, Children 7-12 $8, Under 7: Free

Hours: Sunday – Thursday, 800 am to 600 pm, Friday and
Saturday, 800 am to 800 pm

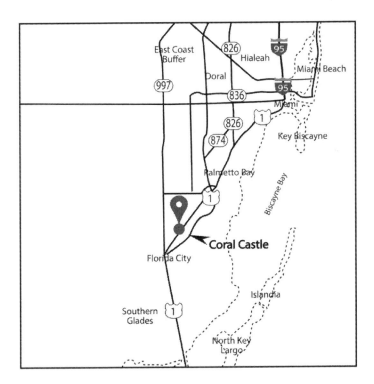

CROSS CREEK

Cross Creek is a tiny town between Ocala and Gainesville that was the home of writer Marjorie Kinnan Rawlings. She wrote "The Yearling" here and other classics and her home is now preserved and operated by the Florida State Park Service. This quiet village is located on the creek that joins Lakes Lockloosa and Orange. Other than Ms. Rawlings home there isn't much to do in Cross Creek but soak up the atmosphere that is Old Florida and that is rapidly disappearing from this fast growing state.

The Yearling Restaurant is an attraction that most visitors to the town want to experience. They have many items on their menu that are native to Florida, and the atmosphere is rustic and comfortable. There are also some fish camps in town with extremely modest cabins for rent in case you want to make a weekend of your trip.

BASIC INFORMATION

Cross Creek is located on County Road 325 between Ocala and Gainesville. It is between US-301 and US-441 and is not far from historic Micanopy. The address of the State Park is 18700 S. CR-325, Cross Creek, FL 32640. Tel: 352-466-3672.

Admission Fees: $3/car if you want to get into the State Park. You drop your money in an "honor box". Guided tours of the house are $3/adult, $2/child, and are available October through July, Thursday through Sunday, except Christmas and Thanksgiving.

Hours: The town is open and free 24 hours/day; the State Park is open daily from 900 am to 500 pm.

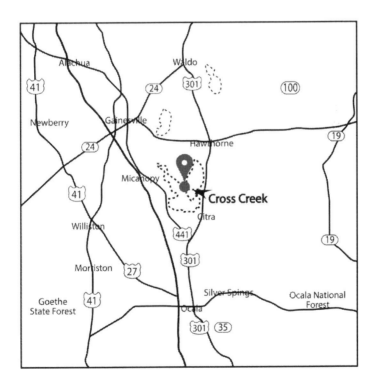

DALI MUSEUM

The Dali Museum will keep you entertained for hours, and you will be amazed out how versatile an artist Salvador Dali was. His fantastic dreamy and warped images are there, but so is his more conventional work that rivals that of the old masters.

The museum is constantly updating its exhibits, and there are guided tours that will give you the inside information on the art you will see. There are also numerous programs so it's best to call the museum in advance to see what' going on.

The architecture itself is a wonder to behold. The futuristic building is on the waterfront near Albert Whitted Airport in downtown St. Petersburg.

The entire family will enjoy this museum.

BASIC INFORMATION

1 Dali Boulevard

St. Petersburg, Florida 33701

Tel: 727-823-3767

thedali.org

Admission Fees: General Admission $24, Children 13-17 $17, Children 6-12 $10, Children 5 and younger free.

Hours: Open 7 days/week 10 am-530 pm, except Thursdays open 1000 am - 800 pm.

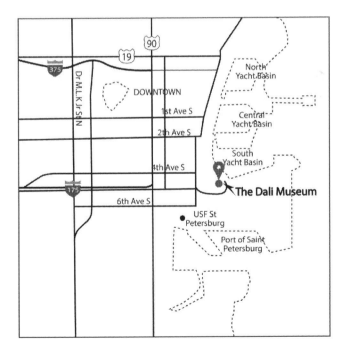

DEFUNIAK SPRINGS

This small panhandle city is a great place to visit because of its large collection of Victorian homes and other buildings surrounding the circular Lake DeFuniak in the historic downtown area. DeFuniak Springs was the summer home from 1885 to 1928 of the Chautauqua Assembly founded in New York State.

All told, there are about 200 historic buildings around the lake and 40 of them are listed on the U.S. National Register of Historic Places. The town only has 8,000 people, so this probably represents the most historic buildings per capita of any town or city in the State of Florida.

The town also has many magnificent old oak trees and many visitors say the town reminds them of New England.

BASIC INFORMATION

The town is located just north of Interstate 10 at the intersection of US-331 and US-90 about 60 miles east of Pensacola and 120 miles west of Tallahassee.

Admission Fees: the town is free for you walk around and look at things to your heart's content.

Hours: Individual attractions, restaurants and other venues have their own hours and prices.

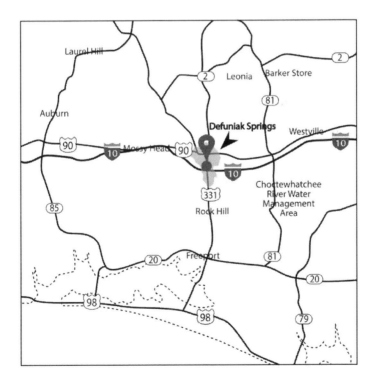

DINOSAUR WORLD

Nobody seem to know for sure why kids are so crazy about dinosaurs, but a visit to this place will convince you they are. You will have a chance to wander around more than 150 replicas of the giant reptiles, displayed in their true size.

Tyrannosaurus Rex is there, of course, along with even scarier creatures you may never have heard of. There is the Boneyard that lets you uncover a life sized dinosaur skeleton. You can also enjoy the Fossil Dig and pretend you are an archeologist.

The movie cave lets you learn about dinosaurs, and there is also a museum, gift shop, and children's playground.

There is plenty of free parking in front of the attraction.

BASIC INFORMATION

5145 Harvey Tew Road

Plant City, Florida 32459

Tel: 813-717-9865

dinosaurworld.com

Admission Fees: $16.95/adult, $11.95/child 3-12,

$14.95/senior, children under 3 free

Hours: Open 365 days/year from 900 am until 500 pm

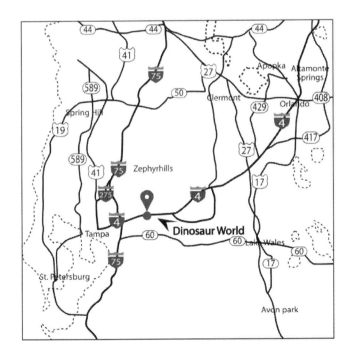

EDISON AND FORD WINTER ESTATES

Thomas Alva Edison was America's greatest inventor and started spending his summers in Fort Myers when he was still in his late 30s. His tough work habits had damaged his health and he was convinced he could get better in Florida.

He chose this site on the Caloosahatchee River in 1885 and spent every winter here until he died in 1931. He did a lot of great work in his Fort Myers laboratory during this 46 year stretch of winters.

Henry Ford got super rich building automobiles and was a good friend of Edison. He bought the property next door to Edison in 1915, and their mutual friend, Harvey Firestone, visited quite often. You will enjoy seeing how these three giants lived and worked in their winter homes.

BASIC INFORMATION

2350 McGregor Blvd

Fort Myers, Florida 33901

Tel: 239-334-7419

edisonfordwinterestates.org

Admission Fees: $20/adult, $15/teen (13-19), $11/child (6-12), children under 6 free.

Hours: 7 days/week 900 am until 530 pm

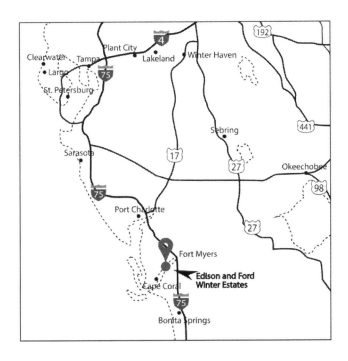

EVERGLADES CITY

Everglades City is about 35 minutes east of downtown Naples. It is a small town of 600 and is a good place to get a feeling for what Old Florida was like before the population explosion of the past 50 years. It was the seat of government of Collier County until Hurricane Donna did tremendous damage in 1960 and the seat was moved to Naples.

The village today makes it living from the nearby salt water and the Florida Everglades. You can enjoy airboat rides in the shallow mangrove waters, and will enjoy taking a peek inside the historic Everglades Rod and Gun Club. It is also a good staging point for visiting Everglades National Park, whose entrance is in Everglades City.

BASIC INFORMATION

Everglades Rod and Gun Club
200 Riverside Drive
Everglades City, Florida 34139
Tel: 239-695-2101

Admission Fees: Everglades City is a town and you can drive around wherever you want.

Hours: Rod and Gun Club and various restaurants have published hours and are open most of the year.

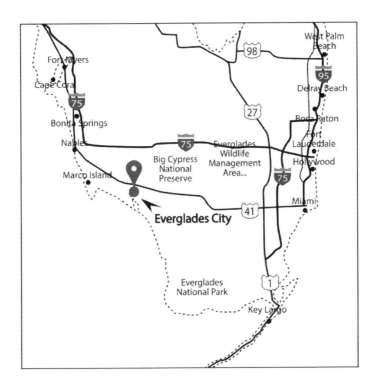

FLORIDA AQUARIUM

Florida Aquarium is ranked in the top 10 aquariums in the United States by TripAdvisor, and it ranks even higher among organizations that determine which aquariums are "kid friendly". The museum has many innovated ways to tell child and adult visitors all about the ecological cycles of Florida's unique water systems.

The aquarium has interactive programs such as "Swim With The Fishes" and "Dive With The Sharks", and other programs let you safely swim with other giant fish and even schmooze with a penguin.

The aquarium also has an outside fun zone with water cannons and other fun things for the kids.

BASIC INFORMATION

701 Channelside Drive

Tamps, Florida 33602

Tel: 813-273-4030

flaquarium.org

Admission Fees: $26.95/adult, $21.95/child (3-11), $22.95/Senior, Children 2 and under free. Parking $6/day

Hours: Daily 930 am to 5 pm, Closed Christmas & Thanksgiving

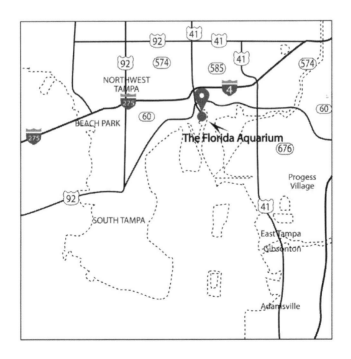

FLORIDA MUSEUM OF NATURAL HISTORY

This museum on the campus of the University of Florida has a collection of natural history that is one of the largest in the United States. Kids especially are fond of the 14 foot mammoth skeleton.

Another feature of this museum that both kids and adults love is the Florida bat cave that has been built inside the museum. You won't be too scared because the bats are not alive.

The museum has the world's second largest collection of Lepidoptera, a specials that includes butterflies. Live butterflies will fly all around you if you pay the small admission fee to get into the Butterfly Rainforest.

The museum charges a small fee for parking in a reserved lot.

BASIC INFORMATION

3215 Hull Road

Gainesville, Florida 32611

Tel: 352-846-2000

flmnh.ufl.edu

Admission Fees: Admission to the museum is free, small parking charge, extra charge for Butterfly Rainforest

Hours: Monday-Saturday, 1000 am- 500 pm, Sunday 1200 pm- 500pm. Closed Thanksgiving and Christmas.

FLORIDA STATE CAPITOL

Tallahassee became the capital of Florida territory back in 1824 and held onto this distinction through Statehood and beyond. The old capitol building has been preserved and restored and is immediately next door to the modern tower that serves as the headquarters for Florida's state government.

You can take a self guided tour. The highlight of a tour is the trip to the top of the 22 story building for a breathtaking view of Tallahassee from the observation deck.

BASIC INFORMATION

400 South Monroe St

Tallahassee, Florida 32399

Tel: 850-488-6167

visitfloridacapitol.com

Admission Fees: Free, guided tours are also available

Hours: Monday through Friday, 800 am to 500 pm, closed on major government holidays.

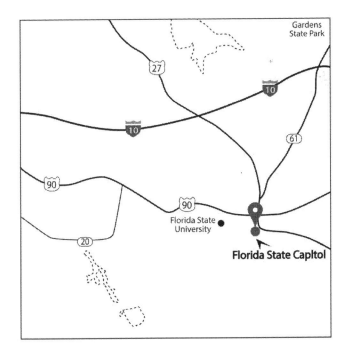

FORT CLINCH STATE PARK

This 1400 acre state park has some beautiful beaches along its 3 mile shoreline. It also has many natural areas for viewing wildlife and also historic Fort Clinch where your hosts are wearing period uniforms and will tell you all about the fort. There is an extra fee of $2/person to enter the fort.

The park has 69 beautiful campsites and is a favorite place for family activities with swimming, fishing, shelling, shark tooth hunting, hiking and biking. There is something for everyone in this well maintained park.

The park has several freshwater ponds that are home to numerous alligators and turtles. There are also saltwater marshes that give you view of the many wading birds that make this park their home.

BASIC INFORMATION

2601 Atlantic Avenue
Fernandina Beach, Florida 32034
Tel: 904-277-7274
www.floridastateparks.org/park/Fort-Clinch

Admission Fees: $6/vehicle, 2-8 people. $4/single occupant vehicle. $2/person fort admission. Camping fee $26/night.

Hours: Open 365 days/year, 900 am to 500 pm (fort)

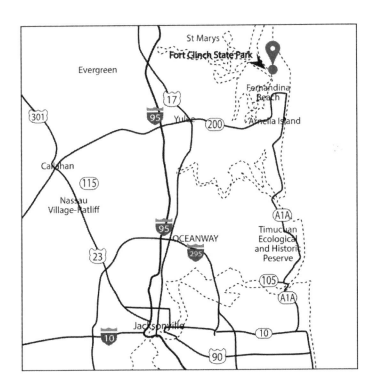

FRUIT AND SPICE PARK

This unique park is operated by Miami-Dade County and is in the heart of one of the most unusual agricultural areas in the world, The Redlands. The area around the park is loaded with farms and fields of tropical vegetables, plants and palm trees. Things grow in the Redlands that don't grow anyplace else.

The park is 40 acres and has more than 500 varieties of herbs, nuts, spices and exotic fruit. The park's plant collection has specimens from all over the world including Hong Kong, Singapore, Burma, Indonesia, Vietnam, Cambodia, Thailand, Malaysia, Phillippines, Panama, Belize, Guatemala, Costa Rica, Hondura, and Mexico.

There is a nice gift shop in the park building where you can sample some of the fruit in the park and buy merchandise made from the products of the park.

BASIC INFORMATION

24801 SW 187th Avenue
Homestead, Florida 33031
Tel: 305-247-5727
fruitandspicepark.org

Admission Fees: Adults $8, Children $2

Hours: Daily 900 am – 500 pm. Closed on Christmas Day

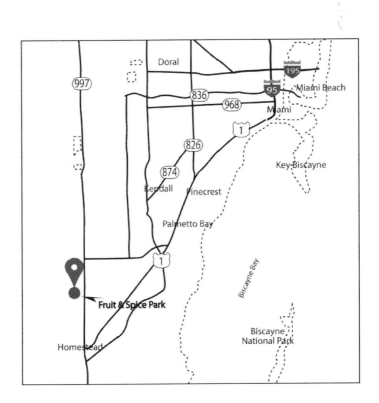

GATORLAND

Gatorland has been thrilling visitors since 1949, a full 22 years before neighboring Walt Disney World opened its doors. It is a place for family fun, and the 110 acre park offers a true glimpse into the "Old Florida" that is so quickly disappearing.

You will see thousands of alligators, some crocodiles (including some white ones), a free-flight aviary, petting zoo and several animal shows. There is even a zip line for an extra charge that will let you soar above the hungry gators.

BASIC INFORMATION

14501 South Orange Blossom Trail

Orlando, Florida 32837

Tel: 800-393-5297

gatorland.com

Admission Fees: $26.99/adult, $18.99/child, under 3 Free.

Hours: Open Daily, 1000 am to 500 pm, free parking.

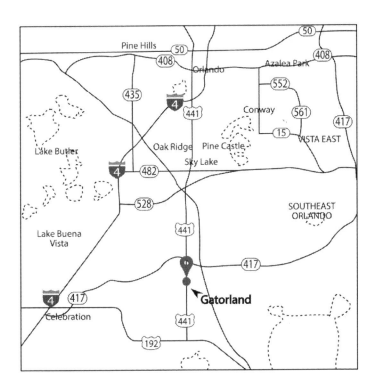

GINNIE SPRINGS

Ginnie Springs is a privately owned park that offers a lot of outdoor activities. You can scuba dive, camp, go canoeing and kayaking, and enjoy the 200 acre natural Florida setting. There are 90 full service campsites on the property, along with picnic tables and grills and bathrooms to serve the campsites.

The water in the springs is crystal clear and even received the ultimate compliment from Jacques Costeau, the father of SCUBA.

Reservations are needed for the campsites, and some of the special adventures, such as cavern and cave diving, require certification on the part of the visitor.

BASIC INFORMATION

5000 NE 60th Avenue

High Springs, Florida 32643

Tel: 386-454-7188

ginniespringsoutdoors.com

Admission Fees: $14.02/adult, $3.73/child (6-14), 5 and under free. Extra fees for scuba diving and camping

Hours: Summer Hours and Winter Hours. Check website.

GRAYTON BEACH STATE PARK

Grayton Beach usually makes everybody's list of the most beautiful and user friendly beaches in the United States. It's great for swimming, chilling out, fishing and just enjoying the sun and surf. The state park itself has 2,000 acres.

There are freshwater lakes so you can enjoy saltwater and freshwater fishing in the same park. You can enjoy canoeing, kayaking, walks along the nature trail through the coastal forest and enjoy riding your bike on other trails. Campsites and cabins are also available.

BASIC INFORMATION

357 Main Park Road

Santa Rosa Beach, FL 32459

Tel: 850-231-4210

www.floridastateparks.org/park/Grayton-Beach

Admission Fees: $5/vehicle (2-8 people/vehicle), $4/single occupant vehicle, $2 pedestrians, bicyclists, extra passengers.

Hours: Open 365 days/year, 800 am to Sundown

Grayton Beach State Park
Oceanfront &
Lakefront activities

HEMINGWAY HOME

In 1931 Key West became the permanent home of Ernest and Pauline Hemingway. Their house was a unique 1851 Spanish Colonial style built from native limestone.

The home was built using limestone from the home site and the resulting pit crated a large basement, rare in the Keys. Another rarity was the swimming pool that Hemingway built for what would be $300,000 in today's money. Ernest kidded his wife about the cost of the pool and said *"Pauline, you've spent all but my last penny, so you might as well have that!"* Visitors can see the penny embedded in among the stones by the pool.

You will probably also see some six toed cats on the property. As you walk around you will undoubtedly notice the many polydactyl cats. For several years after Pauline's death, the home was a museum and home to their beloved and well cared for cats.

The home's interior is filled with European antiques and animal trophies from Hemngway's African safaris.

BASIC INFORMATION

907 Whitehead Street
Key West, Florida 33040
Tel: 386-497-1113
www.hemingwayhome.com

Admission Fees: Adults, $14. Children 6-12 $6, Children under 6 Free

Hours: Open 7 Days/Week 900 am to 500 pm.

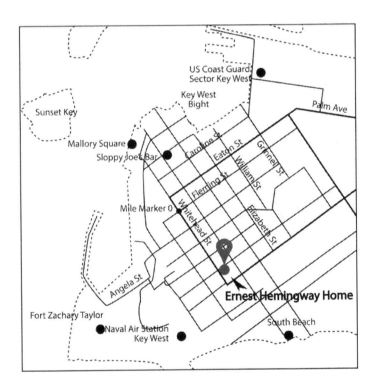

JACKSONVILLE ZOO

This zoo is more than 100 years old and is located on 89 acres on the shore of Trout River north of downtown Jacksonville. The zoo is organized by natural exhibits including River Valley Apiary, African Loop, Stingray Bay, Wild Florida, Savanna Blooms, Great Apes, Giraffe Overlook, Range of the Jaguar.

For the kids, there is also the Play Park and Splash Ground and the ability to pet the stingrays in Stingray Bay.

The Gardens at Trout River Plaza is a large botanical garden that is a place where facilities can be rented for special events.

Kids also love feeding the kangaroos and wallabies at Australian Adventure.

BASIC INFORMATION

370 Zoo Parkway

Jacksonville, Florida 32218

Tel: 904-757-4463

jacksonvillezoo.org

Admission Fees: Adults $17.95, Seniors $15.95, Children 3-12

$12.95, Children Under 3 Free

Hours: Open Monday-Friday 900 am-500 pm, Saturday and

Sunday 900 am – 600 pm. Closed on Christmas

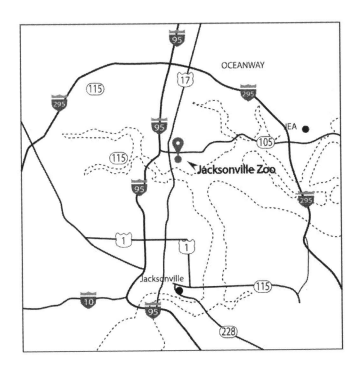

JUNGLE ISLAND

Jungle Island has been around for more than 75 years in one form or another. It was called Parrot Jungle and located south of Miami. It was famous for letting birds fly around without cages. The attraction moved to its current location on downtown's Watson Island in 2003, and changed its name to Jungle Island in 2007.

It is home to more than 2,000 varieties of tropical plants and 1,100 tropical birds. The birds still fly free.

BASIC INFORMATION

1111 Parrot Jungle Trail
Miami, Florida 33132
Tel: 305-400-7000
citrustower.com

Admission Fees: Adults $39.95, Children 3-15 $32.95, Children younger than 3, Free

Hours: Daily, 1000 am to 500 pm.

JUNGLE QUEEN

This riverboat cruise will delight you as you glide along the many miles of waterways in Fort Lauderdale. You will learn all about the history of this great town and see the homes of many rich and famous people.

The boat holds more than 500 passengers and resembles an old Florida paddlewheel steamer from the pioneer days of Florida. The cruise takes 3 hours including a stop at a small island on the New River called Jungle Queen Indian Village. There you will see a man wrestling an alligator.

If you take the cruise in the evening, the Jungle Queen features a buffet dinner. The ride on the vessel is slow and steady.

BASIC INFORMATION

801 Seabreeze Boulevard (Bahia Mar)

Fort Lauderdale, Florida 33316

Tel: 954-462-5596

www.junglequeen.com

Admission Fees: Sightseeing Cruises Adults $23.95-$29.95,

Children $12.95-$14.95. Dinner cruises are more.

Hours: Open Mon 900 am-600pm, Tue 900 am-700 pm,

Wednesday through Sunday 900 am- 730 pm.

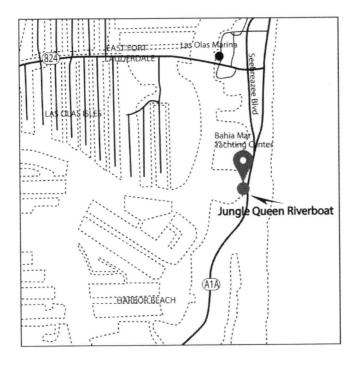

KEY WEST AQUARIUM

The Key West Aquarium was built by the Federal Government's Works Progress Administration in 1932 and what was then the world's only open air aquarium. This is a simple aquarium without a lot of the high tech adventures typical in many modern big city establishments.

One of the goals of the aquarium is to help preserve the natural habitat and animals of the Florida Keys. Part of that effort is the Green Turtle Head Start Program where baby turtles are raised in captivity and prepared for release to the beaches to help their chances of surviving. You will also see many game and reef fish such as barracuda, tarpon, jacks and snook from a two story observation deck.

BASIC INFORMATION

1 Whitehead Street (Mallory Square)

Key West, Florida 33040

Tel: 888-544-5927

keywestaquarium.com

Admission Fees: Adults $16.11, Children 4-12 $9.66, Special Deals for purchasing online.

Hours: Open Daily 900 am to 600 pm.

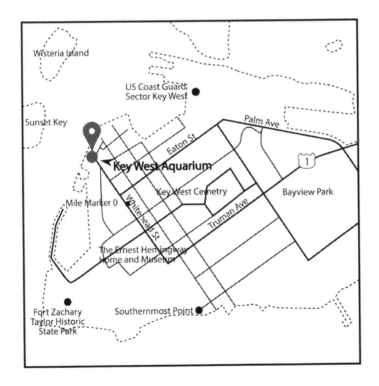

KINGSLEY PLANTATION

Zephaniah Kingsley was an early pioneer in Spanish Florida and began purchasing land in North Florida. His plantation used slave labor and was put into operation in 1814, long before Florida became a territory and U.S. possession.

The National Park Service now owns and operates the old plantation and it offers a glimpse into the life of Kingsley and his slave wife, Anna Madgigine Jai and their four children.

You will get to explore the ruins of 23 coquina and shell cabins that were the slave quarters along with Kingsley's home, the main house. The visitor center and museum are located in this house.

BASIC INFORMATION

11676 Palmetto Avenue

Jacksonville, Florida 32226

Tel: 904-251-3537

www.nps.gov/timu/learn/historyculture/kp_visiting.htm

Admission Fees: Free

Hours: Open 7 Days/Week 900 am to 500 pm except
Thanksgiving Day, Christmas Day and New Years Day.

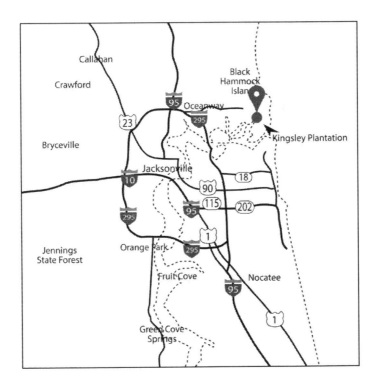

LEU GARDENS

Harry P. Leu Gardens is located in north Orlando on 50 acres of some of the most beautiful botanical gardens in Florida. It has been a popular attraction since 1961 and was the home of the Leu family. They donated it to the City and the gardens have been expanded since then.

The property is divided into more than a dozen specialty gardens connected by sidewalks so you can enjoy self guided tours. The variety of plants is amazing and includes bananas, bromeliads, birds of paradise, cactus, bamboo, herbs, citrus and vegetables. No irrigation is used; all plants are sustained by natural rainfall. Some of their vegetable harvest goes to local food banks, and some is used in cooking classes that are held on the property in the Garden House.

BASIC INFORMATION

1920 North Forest Avenue

Orlando, Florida 32803

Tel: 407-246-2620

leugardens.org

Admission Fees: Adult $10, Child (K-12) $3, 4 and younger Free

Hours: 900 am to 500 pm every day except Christmas. Last admission is at 430 pm.

MICANOPY

This small village south of Gainesville is named after the famous Seminole, Chief Micanopy. Although he didn't live here, the area was home to many Seminoles and there was a lot of fighting during the three Seminole Wars. Today's peaceful Micanopy makes that time seem unreal and far away.

It is essentially a one street town with old buildings providing home to two or three small café's and a few antique shops. The photo above is the Herlong Mansion, a bed and breakfast inn in the heart of town that makes a great place to stay while you are visiting.

The movie "Doc Hollywood" starring Michael J Fox and Woody Harrelson was mostly filmed right here in Micanopy.

BASIC INFORMATION

Micanopy is on the west side of US-441 south of Gainesville. The entire village is a historic district.

Admission Fees: You can visit the town for free. Individual shops and restaurants have varying prices.

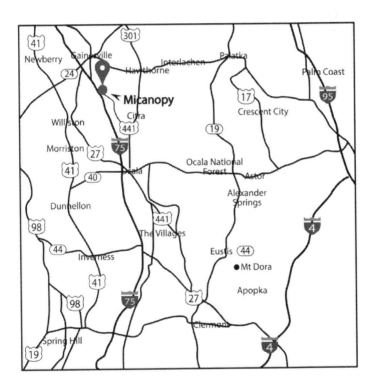

MILL CREEK RETIREMENT HOME FOR HORSES

The people who started the Mill Creek Farm wanted to do something to help old horses that were too old to be ridden or used in various businesses and police departments any longer. They also wanted a place to bring rescued horses that had been abused and saved by the SPCA or other humane societies and concerned people.

The farm has 200 rolling acres of pasture land for the horses to wander around in wherever they'd like. Plenty of trees on the property give the horses welcome shade from the sun. There are about 100 horses living on the farm at any given time. You can have a chance to meet some of them.

BASIC INFORMATION

20307 Northwest County Road 235A
Alachua, Florida 32615
Tel: 386-462-1001
millcreekfarm.org

Admission Fees: Two Carrots/person

Hours: Open Saturday Only 1100 am to 300 pm.

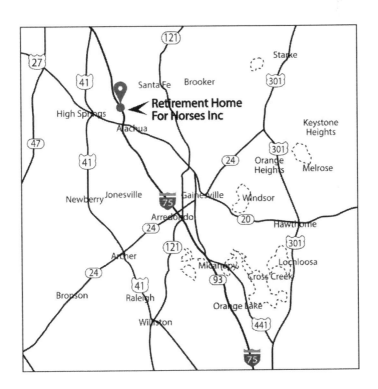

MILTON

Milton is one of Florida's oldest cities and dates back to 1844, the year before Florida became a state. The centerpiece of the town is the Blackwater River and the downtown historic district has many interesting old buildings that give the town its unique flavor.

One of the historic structures is St. Mary's Episcopal Church and Rectory on Oak Street. It was built in 1888 and is mentioned in Frank Lloyd Wright's book "The Aesthetics of American Architecture".

There are several good restaurants in downtown Milton, some on the river, and it is a support town for naval aviation in nearby Pensacola.

BASIC INFORMATION

Milton is located on US-90 where it crosses the Blackwater River about 23 miles northeast of Pensacola. City Hall is located at 6738 Dixon Street in Milton. Tel: 850-983-5400.

Admission Fees: the town is open 24 hours/day and you are free to explore at your will. Various attractions and other venues charge separate admission fees.

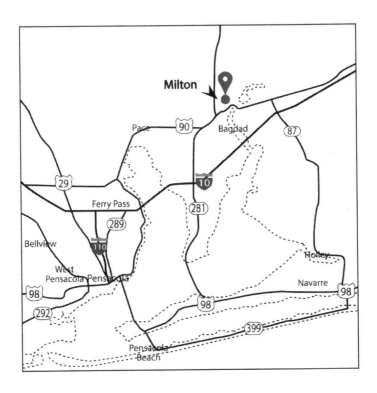

MOUNT DORA

Mount Dora is nestled among the lakes in the hilly country about 45 minutes northwest of downtown Orlando. Its downtown is on the shore of Lake Dora, one of the Harris Chain of Lakes that one time connected Mount Dora by steamship to the larger world outside of Central Florida.

Today the town is known as "The Festival City" because of its many art and craft shows, antique shows, music festivals and dozens of other events. A large antique mall on the east side of town, Renninger's, boasts more than 100 vendors. Downtown Mount Dora has dozens of neat restaurants and gift shops.

One of the lodging opportunities is the Lakeside Inn, the oldest continuously operating hotel in Florida. It's on Lake Dora.

BASIC INFORMATION

510 North Baker Street – City Hall

Mount Dora, Florida 32757

Tel: 352-735-7100

ci.mount-dora.fl.us

Admission Fees: The city is free to visitors all the time. There are many festivals where parking is tightly controlled. Most downtown restaurants stop serving about 9-10 pm

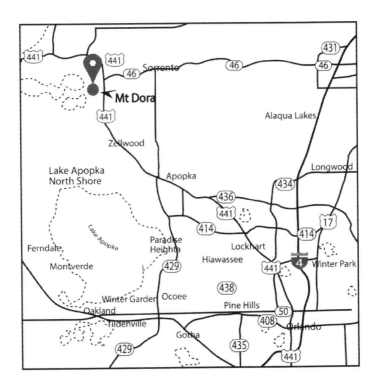

NAPLES ZOO

This zoo was established in 1919 when Naples was still a small settlement on the southwestern frontier of Florida. It was originally established as a botanical garden, which explains its full name of Naples Zoo at Caribbean Gardens. Many of the more than 3,000 plants from the original gardens are still thriving on today's zoo property.

Many animals live in the zoo in habitats designed to enhance their freedom and natural surroundings. One popular fellow is Uno, a Florida panther that was rescued after losing one eye by a blast from a shotgun.

You will see gators, anteaters, bears, cheetahs, snakes, foxes, frogs, gibbons, gila monsters and even a honey badger that the children love to interact with (he's behind very strong glass).

BASIC INFORMATION

1590 Goodlette-Frank Road

Naples, Florida 34102

Tel: 239-262-5409

napleszoo.org

Admission Fees: Adults $22.95, Children 3-12 $14.95, Children under 3 Free. Discounts for Seniors and Military.

Hours: Monday through Sunday 900 am-500 pm, Closed on Thanksgiving and Christmas.

NAVAL AVIATION MUSEUM

U.S. Navy pilots are considered to be among the best aviators in the world and their history is celebrated in this fantastic museum on Naval Air Station Pensacola. You will see more than 150 wonderfully restored airplanes and 4,000 other items related to aviation in the Navy, Marines and Coast Guard.

You can sit in a flight simulator and get a feeling for what it's like to fly a naval aircraft, and you can also enjoy action packed movies in the IMAX theater.

The Flight Deck Store has all kinds of souvenirs and mementoes related to Naval Aviation, and there is also a nice restaurant.

BASIC INFORMATION

1750 Radford Boulevard, Suite C

Naval Air Station Pensacola, Florida 32508

Tel: 850-452-3604

navalaviationmuseum.org

Admission Fees: Free

Hours: Open Daily 900 am to 500 pm. Visitors without Department of Defense ID need to enter via West Gate.

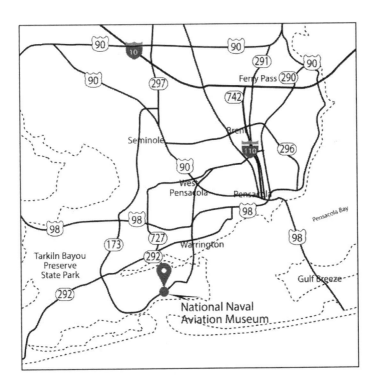

PADDLING ADVENTURES

Paddling Adventures is a facility located within Ichtetucknee Springs State Park that rents single or double kayaks, canoes and standup paddleboards. Floridians for generations have been enjoying inner tube rafting down the crystal clear waters of this spring fed river. They can now rent something other than an inner tube and paddle down the river at their own leisure.

The rental facility is located at the north entrance to the state park on State Road 238. That's where you start your trip and paddle 2.5 miles south past Blue Hole, Devil's Eye, Devil's Den, Coffee Spring and other scenic sites to the Last Takeout Point.

From the take out point, a small bus or van will take you back to where you started and parked your car at the north entrance.

BASIC INFORMATION

12087 Southwest U.S.-27

Fort White, Florida 32038

Tel: 386-497-1113

www.paddlingadventures.com/ichetucknee-springs/

Admission Fees: $6/car to get into the park, $20 to $35 for range of kayaks, canoes and paddle boards.

Hours: Open 7 Days/Week 900 am to 230 pm.

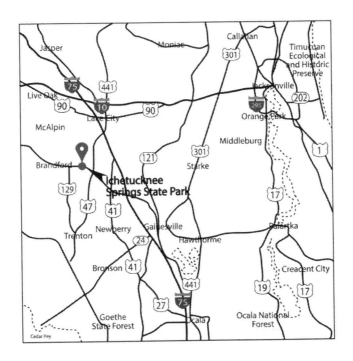

PANAMA CITY

Panama City has become famous – or infamous – as the current location of Spring Break, that madhouse vacation period when college students from all over the country come to town to get drunk and raise hell. Most of the activity takes place on nearby Panama City Beach.

Other times of the year this area becomes a great family vacation paradise. Since it attracts many summer vacationers from nearby Alabama and South Georgia, it is fondly called "The Redneck Riviera" by some politically insensitive folks. It's a great tourist place with lots of affordable attractions for both adults and kids.

BASIC INFORMATION

For information on Panama City attractions, see
www.10best.com/destinations/florida/panama-
city/attractions/best-attractions-activities/

For information on Panama City Beach attractions, see
www.visitpanamacitybeach.com/things-to-do/attractions-and-
entertainment/

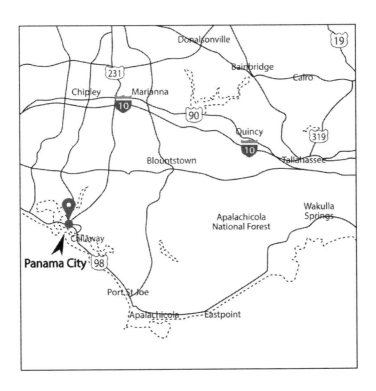

PRINCESS PLACE PRESERVE

This preserve is located on 1500 acres near Palm Coast on the mainland between Daytona and St. Augustine. It is a peaceful place that will give you an idea of what Old Florida was like. One some days the only sounds you will hear are the breathing of the wind through the ancient oak trees and the gentle lapping of the waves of nearby Pellicer Creek.

The lodge on the property was a hunting lodge built in 1886 and the widow of the owner got remarried to an exiled Russian prince. She got the title and he got a rich wife. The lodge is open for tours on Fridays, Saturdays and Sundays. The preserve has some camping spots and horse trails too.

BASIC INFORMATION

2500 Princess Place Road
Palm Coast, Florida 32137
Tel: 386-313-4020
flaglercounty.org/Facilities/Facility/Details/18

Admission Fees: Admission Free, camping is extra.

Hours: Monday-Sunday, 700 am – 600 pm. Lodge tours at
200pm Friday-Sunday.

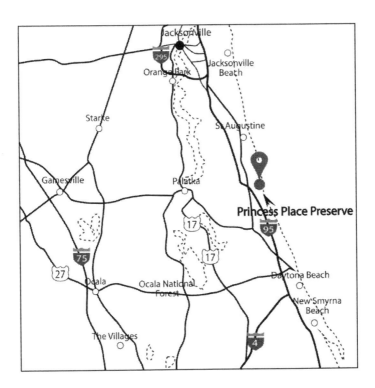

ROBERT IS HERE

Robert started this fruit stand when he was only 6 years old and it has become a popular tourist attraction in the Homestead area south of Miami. It is a produce market that has been providing fruit and produce to local residents and tourists since 1959.

The store is stacked high with fresh vegetables and fruit. You can find tomatoes, papaya, watermelon, oranges, grapefruit, tangerine, corn and more exotic tropical things like carambola, lychee, mangoes and others.

People love Robert's fresh fruit milkshakes and homemade key lime pie. Robert even serves a key lime milkshake.

BASIC INFORMATION

19200 SW 344th Street
Homestead, Florida 33034
Tel: 305-246-1592
robertishere.com

Admission Fees: Free, prices for produce and drinks vary.

Hours: Open daily 800 am – 700 pm November through August.
Closed Sep and Oct. Open Thanksgiving 800 am- 400pm,
Christmas 1200 pm- 700pm.

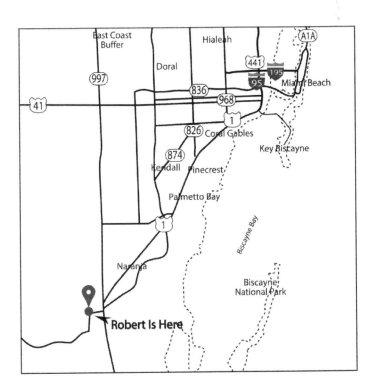

ST AUGUSTINE ALLIGATOR FARM

Not many tourist attractions are on the National Register of Historic Places, but this one is. It was founded in 1893 and has entertained and educated millions of people to the fearful alligator. This zoo also has hundreds of species of birds, monkeys, snakes, lions, turtles, and it even has porcupines and tarantulas.

The attraction also has a zip line where you can soar over the alligators and imagine them licking their chops over you.

BASIC INFORMATION

999 Anastasia Boulevard
St. Augustine, Florida 32080
Tel: 904-824-3337
alligatorfarm.com

Admission Fees: Adults $23.99, Children 3-11 $12.99, Other discounts described on website.

Hours: Open daily 900 am – 500 pm, open one hour longer in summer.

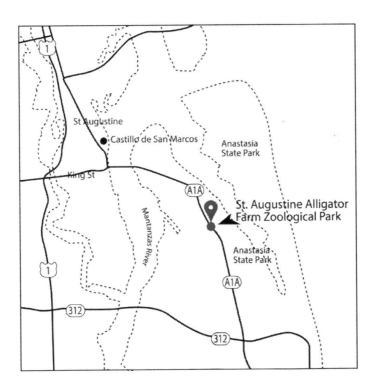

SEASIDE

Seaside is a planned community that was created in 1981 on what had been an 80 acre private family retreat near Seagrove Beach. The community is a pioneer of the concept now known as New Urbanism. Seaside has spurred the development of several hundred similar communities in Florida and elsewhere. It was also the setting for the movie the "Truman Show".

The town is designed for pedestrians. You can park your car and wander all over town on trails and sidewalks. The houses and other buildings are typical of Old Florida with wide overhanging roofs, porches, and wood frame construction.

BASIC INFORMATION

Seaside is on the Gulf of Mexico on State Road 30A about halfway between Panama City and Fort Walton Beach. There are several restaurants there as well as at least three inns. Parking is a problem in season (spring and summer).

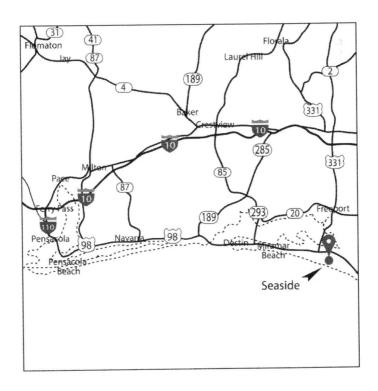

Seaside

SOLOMON'S CASTLE

Howard Solomon was a renowned sculptor who lived and worked in this unique place in the middle of nowhere. He made the castle out of discarded silver colored printing plates and also decorated it with 90 stained glass windows he made himself. His original property was a 40 acre swampy parcel and it's amazing what he's done with it.

The main floor is where you can see his galleries loaded with hundreds of sculptures made out of what most people would consider to be junk. He had a gift for creating beautiful art out of this junk and had mastered the skills of welding, painting, carpentry, and wood turning. Howard passed away in 2016 but his family still owns and operates the attraction.

BASIC INFORMATION

4533 Solomon Road

Ona, Florida 33865

Tel: 863-494-6077

solomonscastle.org

Admission Fees: $12.95/adult, $5 children 12 and under, cash only no credit cards accepted.

Hours: Tuesday-Sunday, 1100 am to 400 pm, Oct 1-Aug 1

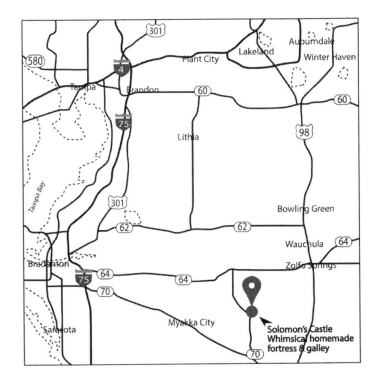

STEINHATCHEE SCALLOPING

Scalloping season runs from the Saturday before July 1 until September 24. If July 1 is a Saturday then that is the opening date. During season, thousands of people gather along the gulf coast from south of Steinhatchee area up to the Carrabelle area. Their fishing equipment consists of snorkel gear and buckets.

A saltwater fishing license is required to harvest the tasty little critters unless you wade into the shallow waters and feel for the animals with your feet and hands without using a mask or snorkel. It's easier and more fun to buy a license at one of the local businesses. You can also rent a boat in Steinhatchee or ask a local where the best location is for wading.

BASIC INFORMATION

Several businesses can help you go scalloping, including selling you a license. One is Steinhatchee Landing Resort.

Tel: 352-498-3513 , Website: steinhatcheelanding.com

Admission Fees: $17/person for fishing license. Food and lodging prices vary in local establishments.

STEPHEN FOSTER STATE PARK

This park is on the Suwannee River, the inspiration for Stephen Foster's classic song "Old Folks at Home". The museum in the park features exhibits about Foster, and you will hear his music singing from the parks 97 bell carillon during your visit.

This is a folk center, so you can watch demonstrations of blacksmithing, quilting, stainless glass art, and browse through the large gift shop.

There are miles of trails winding through beautiful wooded North Florida countryside and you can ride your bike or enjoy hiking.

There is also a full facility campground in the park, or you can stay in a cabin. Every Memorial Day weekend, the park is host to the famous Florida Folk Festival. The park also has several special events during the year.

BASIC INFORMATION

11016 Lillian Sanders Drive

White Springs, Florida 32096

Tel: 386-397-2733

floridastateparks.org/park/Stephen-Foster

Admission Fees: $5/vehicle (2-8 people), $4 single occupant vehicle, $2 pedestrians, bicyclists, extra passengers

Hours: 800 am to Sunset. Check website for special hours.

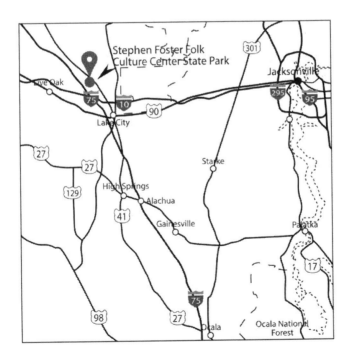

TOPSAIL HILL DUNES STATE PARK

This park gets its name from the majestic high sand dunes that looked like the sails on ships to early mariners on the Gulf of Mexico. It has some of the most beautiful beaches in the world, and the highest dunes in Florida.

The beach is 3 miles long and is among many things you can do in this park. There are 3 coastal dune lakes for fishing, and plenty of areas for bird watching among the long leaf pines, pine scrub and wetlands. There is also a nearby RV resort with a swimming pool and other amenities.

BASIC INFORMATION

7525 West Scenic Highway 30A

Santa Rosa Beach, Florida 32459

Tel: 850-267-8330

floridastateparks.org/hours-and-fees/Topsail-Hill

Admission Fees: $6/vehicle (2-8 people), $4 single occupant vehicle, $2 pedestrians, bicyclists, extra passengers

Hours: Open 365 days/year from 800 am until Sundown

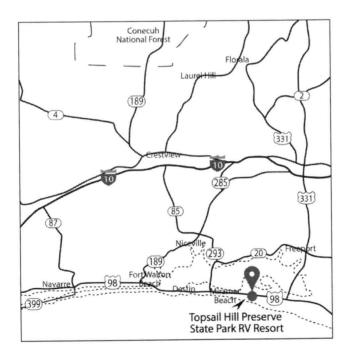

WEBSTER FLEA MARKETS

Webster is one of Florida's quietest small villages except for Mondays, the one day of the week the flea markets are open. The busiest time here is during the winter when all the snowbirds have come back down to Florida. During those months, more than 4,000 vendors are on site selling their goods to as many as 100,000 shoppers.

There are large parking lots that are close to the several flea markets. In addition to flea market items like tools, hats, towels, sheets, lotion, jewelry and other goodies, you will see a huge farmer's market with dozens of tomatoes, onion, peppers, squash and anything else that grows in Florida.

BASIC INFORMATION

Webster Westside Flea Market

516 Northwest Third Street

Webster, Florida 33597

websterwestsidefleamarket.com

Admission Fees: Free, restaurants charge extra

Hours: Open year round but only on Monday, 500 am to 300 pm (Oct-Apr), 600 am to 200 pm (May-Sep)

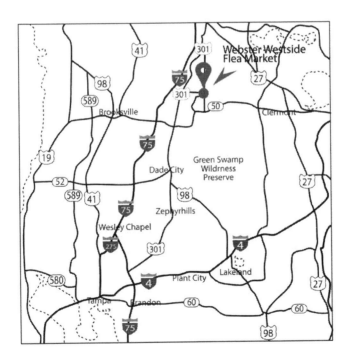

WEEKI WACHEE SPRINGS

Weeki Wachee Springs and its mermaid show was one of Florida's earliest pre-Disney attractions. It fell into financial problems in the years after Disney opened, but is now part of the Florida State Park System. This saved the attraction, and you will be glad it did.

Mermaid shows are still being held, and Buccaneer Bay has been added, a water attraction with a giant slide that opened more than 30 years ago. Don't be surprised if you see other Florida natives swimming with the mermaids. Turtles, fish, manatees, otters and even an occasional gator show up now and then. You can also rent inner tubes and drift down the river. Kayaks and canoes are also available to rent.

BASIC INFORMATION

6131 Commercial Way

Spring Hill, Florida 34606

Tel: 352-592-5656

weekiwachee.com

Admission Fees: $13/adult, $8/child (6-12), 5 and under free.

Mermaid shows, boat ride included in admission fee.

Hours: 900 am to 530 pm, 365 days/year

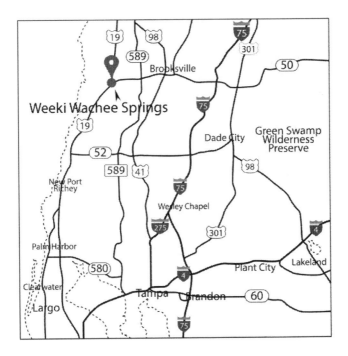

WINTER PARK SCENIC BOAT TOUR

The Winter Park Scenic Boat Tour has been entertaining visitors since 1938. It is only a one hour attraction, but you will have plenty of fun during that hour. The pontoon boats cruise on a route between Lakes Osceola, Virginia and Maitland and go past some of the most expensive real estate in Florida.

You will see many tropical trees and plants along the route, especially in the canals that connect the lakes. You will also learn about the famous structures in Winter Park history and who lived there then and who lives there now.

The tour guides are local captains who know the lake area well and keep you interested from beginning to end.

BASIC INFORMATION

312 East Morse Boulevard

Winter Park, Florida 32789

Tel: 407-644-4056

scenicboattours.com

Admission Fees: $14/adult, $7/child (2-11), special group rates

Cash or checks only.

Hours: Every day except Christmas, 1000 am – 400 pm

61832309R00061

Made in the USA
Columbia, SC
26 June 2019